The Beauty Shop World at a Glance

The Beauty Shop World at a Glance

HAZEL BOGARD

How to Keep Clients Forever
How to Lose Clients Forever

...A BOOK EVERY HAIR STYLIST SHOULD HAVE

Outskirts Press, Inc.
Denver, Colorado

The Beauty Shop World at a Glance
How to keep clients forever how to lose clients forever..... A book every hair stylist should have
All Rights Reserved.
Copyright © 2011 Hazel Bogard
Author Photo, Cover, & Cover Images by Leslie "Tremane" Edwards. Used with permission.
v1.0

Outskirts Press, Inc.
http://www.outskirtspress.com

ISBN: 978-1-4327-7042-6

Outskirts Press and the "OP" logo are trademarks belonging to Outskirts Press, Inc.

PRINTED IN THE UNITED STATES OF AMERICA

Contents

Preface

MY INTENT IN writing this book is to assist hair stylists in creating a clientele that will be with them forever and eliminate forever losing clients. It is based on delivering good customer service, and knowing what patrons want and expect.

After being in the cosmetology field for several years, I felt the need to share not only my personal experiences regarding customer service, but other patrons' experiences, who shared them with me to include in this book.

My journey consists of visits to several hair stylists while also interviewing patrons who were eager to share their "one time" visits. It is my hope and desire that stylists and those who are aspiring to become stylists will use this book as a learning mechanism for creating lasting relationships with clients and building a solid clientele.

This book features guidelines for learning what can prevent a business from growing into a successful career. Last but not least, this book will definitely benefit cosmetology schools around the world! When a student receives their license and is aware of how to be successful, their journey to keeping clients forever will start with confidence!

Once you start reading this book, you will not put it down until you have finished!

Acknowledgements

FIRST OF ALL, I would like to thank my mother, Hazel Fingers, for not only encouraging me, but for her prayers as well. Also, for all the great meals she prepared so I could have more time to write. Mother, you are a jewel and one of God's many blessings!

I want to thank my sons, Tremane, Quinyon, Demetrius and Cory for their encouragement. I love you, boys!

Special thanks to my youngest son, Tremane, who is creative, innovative, and, an excellent illustrator. I challenged him to design my book cover and he exceeded my expectations. I commend you, son, for a job well done.

To my siblings, Ike, Victor, Debra, and Veronica: I thank them for their support, even though it may have caught them by surprise; they knew baby sister was eager and willing to share her personal experiences while helping others as well.

Then I would like to thank William Slade for supporting me when I brought up the idea of this book. After sharing many of my experiences, he immediately knew that I was the right person for the job.

I want to thank Rosemary Thomas for her editing expertise and her advice and suggestions for clarity. She spent several days reviewing and assisting while never giving up on me. She is truly a blessing!

Nathan McMurray, thank you for that extra push I needed to finalize my book. You are appreciated!

My best friend, Sonja McKinley, who has stood beside me through this entire process while supporting me throughout the years of writing this book. Thank you for always being there.

Last but not least, the people I interviewed—Rosemary Thomas, Marshell Johnson, Annie Bolton, Cynthia Bogard, Janice Towns, Patricia Newsome, and Sonja McKinley—were eager to talk about their experiences in various hair salons. Also, Marcus Smith, Neomia Mason, and Fabian Muhammad: thank you for your added support.

Hopefully, identifying these particular issues will help eliminate future frustrations for others, while also acknowledging the importance of providing and receiving good customer service while maintaining healthy hair.

Thank you for your time.

Hazel Bogard

1

My Journey for a Stylist Begins (2005-2006)

ALL WOMEN LOOK forward to being pampered, but one thing we love most of all is having our hair looking its best. We look forward to a fresh hairdo because we know everything else will follow, from the makeup, nails, clothes, and don't forget a lot of attitude.

Hello. I am that person mentioned above! Once my hair is done, everything else does follow. I loved styling my own hair so much, I was inspired to go to beauty school for my license, and yes, I received it. After staying in this field about four years, I decided to take on another career, which still deals with customer service. One thing I found out quickly about the hair business is that time and quality service do matter. We live our entire day around time, and we always look forward to good customer service wherever we may go, especially when we are spending our hard-earned money. So when I pursued this career, I wanted my clients to have the best service possible. I wanted them to walk in knowing the chair was waiting for them. Believe me, that will put a smile on their face quickly because they know right away that chair is waiting for them!

Once a client is in that chair, he or she should be your main focus. No one else. It is *their time*!

I immediately found out that it's not always about the money. Why have five clients coming in close to the same time? After juggling them around—yes, I said juggle—the next thing you know, you have clients upset from the wait because you have one in your chair, two under the dryer, one conditioning, and another waiting. Now at this point, it's all about you and making as much money as you possibly can. It's not about the client.

If the client does not say anything to you regarding the services, believe me, they are thinking about it. If you do not see that client again, you know something went wrong. Now, if you continue to overlook this matter when clients do not return, you will never build a steady clientele that will be with you forever. Please believe me when I say don't have a client for the first time, because that will definitely be her last time. I have experienced one-time visits to several hair stylists because of this. Remember, the first impression is a lasting one, and the majority of times, you will not get a second chance. You will be out there advertising your business constantly.

I have always had a problem when trying to find the right stylist. A stylist should want to treat her clients the way she would want to be treated. That has been a very long journey for me. Let me take you down memory lane. Here we go.

Have you ever asked to get your hair trimmed (ends cut only) and got an actual haircut? Well, this does happen more regularly than you think. Actually I hear this happens quite often. A hair stylist should always make sure they are communicating with their client while they are sitting in that chair. If the ends are so damaged that it needs to have more than an average trim, inform the client of this. Do not wait until afterward and say you needed to cut more off. Let them give the okay, and you will not have to worry about any problems later when it may come as a shock to your client. Once the hair is cut off, you cannot go back and put the hair on, unless of course it is a weave.

May 2005

I have had a relaxer for some time, and, boy, did I thank the Lord when they first came out back in the '70s because I am a very tender-headed person with true nappy, coarse hair. I'm sure a lot of you can agree with me on this—straight hair is more manageable if you prefer this type of look, or perms and texturizers if you prefer the curly look. What's important is what pleases you!

Now back to my journey.

May 2005

Well, it was time for a relaxer retouch, and in the chair I went. My hair was being basted (applying oil to the scalp); at least that's what I was thinking because she was parting my hair with her fingers quickly and making sure it was really basted well. Remember, it's not always necessary to baste, but I assumed this was what this person normally did. I noticed that this person was now putting the product all over my head. Now, I was actually thinking this in my mind because I was completely turned away from the mirror. But anyway, she was doing everything with her hands and never picked up any instrument or comb for applying or smoothing. The next thing I heard was "You have been using a no-lye relaxer, so I am making sure I relax it well."

This person had relaxer all over my head, as if my hair had never relaxed, from the roots to the ends. What I originally thought was base turned out to be relaxer all the time. The parting was done with the fingers, and the product was applied with no hair instruments at all. I was devastated and in disbelief. And yes, I lost some of my hair throughout the following months. This was a disaster! Of course I never returned to this person. I had to nurse my hair back to health, which took a long time.

I did my own hair for a year after this incident. Let me say again, everyone loves to be pampered by having someone do their hair, so yes, I was still searching for that someone, so off on my journey I went.

2006

Next stop. I spoke with another stylist while waiting in a salon where my son gets his hair cut, and I was pleased to find out about the products she used and that she specialized in promoting healthy hair. Healthy hair! Wow, was I excited!

That's all I want is healthy hair, and of course if it's healthy it will look good. A few days later I called her and made an appointment.

All right, the day had arrived and off I went. The stylist had a couple of clients there already and I was saying, Okay, I will be patient and wait. And wait I did, and eventually, finally sitting in her chair, I had a smile on my face because it was MY TIME! But in reality it was my time and others'. Well, the relaxer was applied correctly—hey, I was a stylist, I know—but anyway I was in heaven at that point and I was saying, This is it! I found my stylist! I was there two hours or more but I dealt with it. I finally came out with a flawless look and much attitude.

Next stop, can you believe the same stylist!

On this day I was really happy to arrive and see no one there but me. The chair was waiting for me to sit down because it was My Time!

Everything was going pretty smoothly at this point. My hair was wrapped and ready to go under the dryer. If you know anything about wraps, you know normally it takes awhile, depending on the thickness of your hair. So I assumed she would have come to check on me to maybe loosen my hair a bit so the heat from the dryer would go to the roots. Normally this is done before the dryer stops, but maybe not with some stylists.

But when she returned after an hour and loosened my hair, she said I needed to stay under there twenty more minutes.

People, it does not take my hair long to dry because it's thin, and long.

I must make you aware that during this time, the stylist was having a conversation with another stylist nonstop.

I decided then I would not sit under the dryer the entire extended time, so I got up and returned to her chair. At this point the stylist saw me because the person she was talking with was right across from her room. She said to me that she would be right with me. Now wait a minute! Did you hear that? This person did not stop the conversation for at least 10 to 15 minutes. How inconsiderate and very unprofessional.

The stylist finally started back on my head and I told her she could just comb my hair down so I could leave.

That was my last visit. Now remember, I was the only client. I should have been priority.

I have shared with you some of my stories, but actually I want you to hear what I have heard from other patrons and their stories. But before I begin, I must say this: We do have great hair stylists out there who do a good job and take time into consideration, but we have so many who don't, and believe me, it's so hard out there to find that perfect one.

My former clients have called me on several occasions just to see if I have started back to doing hair, and it hurts me to tell them I have not, because I know what they are going through. Sometimes you have to go through so many bad ones to find the right one; but will you have any hair left by then?

Have you ever been in a store or just out and about and you are approached by a stylist advertising her business and she gives you her business card? Well, let me tell you that presentation is everything. Make sure that your own hair is in order even when you are actually working on a client's head. Did you know that potential clients really look at the overall picture, which includes your hair, attitude, the products you use, and your professionalism? Yes, that is true.

I need to get back to the juggling stylist, and yes, that's what I said. Remember earlier I spoke about having several clients going at one time. Some people may be better at this than others, but have you ever had your head shampooed and you were left there in the sink with your head hanging for an extended amount of time? Now you may have conditioner on your head and need for it to saturate for a while, but sometimes this gives the stylist time to maybe roll someone or to finish a style; this is okay, but please not for an hour! And if a client goes to sleep either under the dryer or at the shampoo bowl, don't take advantage of this by extending their wait time. It's not fair.

While we are talking about shampooing, if you have long fingernails, do not dig in the scalp with your nails. Nails can leave an abrasion on the scalp, and actually it's not sanitary to do so.

You know what I love about having a good shampoo? It's the massage that goes along with it. I know someone just had a thought cross their mind, saying, "I don't have time for that." Come on, take some time and surprise your client. She will be in awe. Believe me when I say a stimulating massage to the scalp not only promotes hair growth, but it definitely makes you forget about stress you may have had that day. A shampoo is the beginning of a voyage to your destination of looking and feeling beautified. Wow! I see the turquoise blue water now in the Bahamas and I am running slowly while my hair is flowing in the wind. Sorry, I drifted off. But hey, you know you want to go there with me.

Sometimes just go out of the way with your client with special treatment. You may just get an extra tip but more than that, a happy client.

There are times when a stylist has just enough clients without needing any more, but sometimes greed will sneak in. This reminds me of the time when I started doing hair. It was on the Saturday before Easter, which has got to be the busiest hair day of the year. I started at 7 a.m. and finished around 12:30 am. That's 17 hours. I believe I quit not too long afterward. Anyway, I definitely let the thought of making a lot of money in one night get the best of me, my sleep, time with my boys, and I was unable to even think about focusing on the sermon on Sunday morning.

After this, I decided that I was being unfair to myself and my clients. I did a complete turnaround. From that point on I made time more valuable for both. I made sure that when a client arrived for their scheduled appointment, the chair would be waiting for them, and if I was running behind, the client would wait no longer than 15 minutes.

If a client is running late, it's only fair that they must reschedule; they are given a time to be there, and if they are unable to make it at that time, this will cause your schedule to be thrown off. And once that happens, it's hard or impossible to catch up. You may think I'm being critical, but there must be guidelines to follow in any business.

Finally let's hear some other stories from patrons I have spoken with in regards to their visits to salons.

2

"The Talkative Stylist"

I THOUGHT THIS title was perfect for the stylist who talks entirely too much.

Well, this patron who we will call Rosie states that it is so annoying when your stylist is talking to practically everyone in the shop. This particular visit, the stylist was talking so much and was not attentive to what he was doing while having curling irons in his hands, and he eventually burnt Rosie on the forehead. Wow! This has got to be one of the worst things you can do, to have a client not return. Remember, that mark on her forehead is a reminder of you, because it's not going anywhere anytime soon, thanks to you.

If you have to communicate with anyone in the room and you have a curling iron or any heated instrument in your hand, you should immediately stop when you get a chance and take the instrument away from the head. PUT THE INSTRUMENT DOWN before you do anything else. Some people can't do two things at once, especially me, and also when you hear constant talking or loud voices, it ruins your relaxation.

Secondly, you don't want to hear a lot of the conversations that are going on, and most times if you are doing a lot of talking with others, it's going to slow you down. Come on, y'all, let's be considerate! I know some clients love to get involved with conversations, but believe me, most of them do not.

This brings me to another point. Let's respect our elders and senior citizens at all times. Their ears are sensitive and we really want to treat them with the utmost respect. I just love my seniors; they are like precious babies once again. They mostly just want their hair to be pretty and enjoy this time of special attention. Let's always go that extra mile with them. They deserve it.

Here is some more advice for the talkers: If you are talking to your client and she replies with a brief answer and never adds any more to the conversation, this means "SHUT UP, I DON'T WANT TO BE BOTHERED." Sorry, but I had to go there, and you need to know! The client may have her eyes closed and be totally enjoying the experience; she is probably on a cruise ship watching the waves go by while someone approaches her and asks, "Where have you been all my life?"—but no… you had to interrupt with something that doesn't pertain to her hair before she found out the gentleman's name on the cruise ship. That dream may never come again.

Remember, all clients are different and don't ever expect them to be the same.

3

Telephone Talkers

LET'S GET TO the telephone talkers since we are on this subject. I am aware that you do get calls from clients throughout the day, unless you are the one who continues to burn people. You may not get many, but anyway, I know you definitely want to book them in your appointment book. If you have a client who's in the chair, just politely excuse yourself to take down the information, but this does not mean hold an entire conversation. The person in the chair should have your attention.

Now what about the personal calls? I'm so glad you asked. You cannot hold a conversation on the phone while working on a client. That is so rude. I have seen stylists stay on the phone an extended amount of time. Please stop. This is what I call a guaranteed client loser if it goes on constantly.

4

The Cutters

I MUST SAY, there are some stylists who can cut hair in the perfect style! There is nothing like a good haircut. When you get a good haircut you will have no regrets of losing hair, but when you get a bad one, yes, you know where I'm going with this.

My best friend, who I will call Sandra, has beautiful, thick, shoulder-length hair. I have always cut her hair, but she now resides in another state. She had been searching for the right stylist to give her the layered cut that I had been giving her for years. A stylist was recommended and off she went. One thing she noticed was that the stylist kept going over her cut and cutting more and more off. Afterward she insisted on putting curls in her head. Now Sandra never wears curls, only wraps so her hair can flow, and she has always received never ending compliments on her hair; this sister has beautiful hair.

After a day or so the curls wore off, and it became evident that the curls were for a reason. To hide the mistakes! She was so disappointed and decided to call the owner of the shop to voice her complaint. The owner had her come back and stated she would get her haircut in shape by doing it herself. Would you believe this just added more pain to the injury? It was worse. She never returned to the shop.

First, if you claim to be a great cutter, you may want to have some pictures of your work, and not from magazines. Prove yourself, because you may have to with clients who have had problems with bad cutters. If you know you are good, then you have no problem showing them.

5

My Journey Continues (2008-2009)

2008

SORRY, EVERYONE, I must interrupt the next story to give you an important message. Wow, that sounds like a news bulletin, but guess what? It's great news for me. I just found the stylist I've been longing for! Actually she was referred by a colleague. What really stunned me about this person was that she reminded me of me.

When I arrived for my first visit, I was the first client of the day. I felt like I was sitting on a throne and all eyes were on me, everyone wishing that they were in my place. Now that says a whole lot. She relaxed my hair professionally, and with just the movement of her hands, I sensed so much caring. She really loves what she does and she focuses on perfection.

As I was lying back in the sink bowl, she started washing my hair, and I thought I saw God! It was an amazing adventure. I was thinking in my mind, and almost spoke it, I didn't want to go home that day! Who could blame me! You know what I've been through. I was so excited, I couldn't wait to get to the cutting phase. I'd needed a good trim for a long time. I told her what I wanted, and guess what? It was achieved! More so, I was out of there within an hour and 15 minutes. So, I received a relaxer, a cut, and superb service, and guess what? I have made her my permanent stylist. I can't help but tip her on each visit because I'm well pleased. She is indeed one of my blessings. Thank you, Jesus! At last!

As of now, I have been her client for at least six months and counting, but I must add, she informs me of how my hair is progressing. On my first visit, I expected to have my hair cut shorter than usual since I hadn't had anyone to take care of my trims in years. After my latest visit, I noticed my hair was healthier. Now, with the perfect cut and all that follows, my hair is ready to grow like crazy. If you don't know by now, some men do love long hair, and my gentleman friend is very attentive to hair, period. He loves it as much as I do, so in reality my stylist has pleased two people. Grow, hair, grow!!

I'm sure I'm not the only one who feels like this when they find that perfect stylist. Just think, there are so many patrons out there who have given up on us, so we must evaluate how we run our business. Do we want to make an impression on each and every one of our clients or be selective?

Everyone, I just returned from a short vacation, spending some time with friends. Hey, I had to take a break. Anyway, I'm sorry to say, I have a very sad story to tell. My friend, who I will call Patrice, apparently had the worst hair nightmare on earth, and it is extreme to me. First, let me say, I actually saw Patrice about four months ago and I recall complimenting her on her hair. This sister has always had a beautiful head of hair, cut in a short, tapered style, since I have known her as a teenager. When I saw her this time, my girl had a full wig on! I looked at her twice to make sure this was what I was actually seeing. She practically could not talk without tears flowing from her eyes. We went to a private area within the house so I could take a look, and after she took off the wig, oh my gosh! My eyes were teary. She had bald spots from her forehead to the back nape of her head. Let me just say, there were bald spots all over her head.

To this day, I'm not sure what happened to her hair; I'm not sure if it was chemicals or what, but I had to ask her what type of relaxer was used on her hair , and she had no idea. Now to me, knowing the type of relaxer is very important. I have seen on occasions that there are no labels on product, which means they do not want you to know the brand name, but you have the right to know what's being used.There are some relaxers that I don't particularly care for, since I've had bad experiences with some. I plan to follow up with Patrice during my next visit to my hometown to see if her hair has improved since this tragic incident. Believe me, losing hair is tragic, especially when not planned.

Sorry to cut in on other patrons' stories, but I must bring you back to me. I told you earlier about the stylist I found who reminded me of me—well, I have been disappointed again. Here is my story.

I arrived on a Saturday for a change and other clients were there, so I ended up waiting at least 30 to 45 minutes, but that was fine. I could tell she may have had too many in at one time, but my patience continued and finally I was called in for my relaxer. It was applied, and washed out, but this time, she placed me directly under the dryer so she could start on another client.

First of all, she never places me under the dryer with the style I usually get, which is a blow dry and flat iron. My appointment was before this client, but she completely finished her before finishing me first, which means I sat under the dryer at least 45 minutes. When she finally started back on my hair, she was doing it in a rush and did not have my hair looking like it normally does. It was so dry and dull, I ended up redoing it myself, which means I lost money on this day and relaxers are not cheap. First, there should have been an apology for not taking me on time, and secondly you never change how you do a person's hair if she has been pleased with it.

Now this is what really gets me. After I decided not to return to this stylist, I never received a call personally to find out why I hadn't returned. Hmmmm, how odd. If you never know why a person has not returned who has been a regular, how will you ever know the cause of losing a client? I'm guessing there is a sense of *I don't care*, pride, or someone will eventually replace the person. It's mind-boggling to me because this is where good customer service comes in different categories of a business. I personally would want to know because if it is for other reasons than me, I can let it pass, but if it's about my service, tell me.

April 2009

Hey, everyone, guess what! A new salon has just opened in my neighborhood conveniently around the corner from my home. My birthday is approaching soon and of course I want to have someone, other than myself, relax and style my hair, so off I go again.

I walked in and the atmosphere seemed to be laid back, which really caught my attention. There were at least five stylists in my view and it took at least a few minutes before I was approached by a young lady. I was beginning to think that no one needed a client or they possibly thought that I was someone else's client, but still no "hello" from anyone, which was quite weird to me. *My, aren't you critical*, I'm sure you are thinking, but no, it's just good customer service, especially when you have a sign outside that says "walk-ins welcomed," so don't take a chance or assume until you actually know.

After a stylist approached me and introduced herself, she proceeded to walk me around when I told her I just stopped in to possibly find a stylist to do my hair in the near future. She didn't have any cards, but there were some business cards for the salon if I needed to call and make an appointment.

A few weeks went by and I made an appointment for a relaxer. The day I arrived, she was apparently running late and had not made it in yet. I sat and waited about ten minutes and another stylist informed me that she had called and was on her way, which was acceptable. When she walked in she immediately apologized and stated she was working on getting her own personal salon and was working on her paperwork, which was understandable.

It's always great to hear about people, especially our younger generation, who are eager to get out and have their own business. This is something that I definitely push. When you are your own boss, you make the rules and guidelines. In my own words, you are the president, vice president, CEO, and founder of your business. I just love the way that sounds and you should too.

Well, this person actually basted my scalp, and I am sure this time because I was looking at her through a full-length mirror. Remember the stylist in my story earlier who I thought was basting and actually applied relaxer from the roots to the ends? Oh my gosh, every time I mention that, I get upset all over again, so let me continue.

The applying went well, and off to the sink I went. Oh! Did I mention I was the only client? Yippee! She shampooed my hair and shampooed my hair and shampooed my hair. Did I tell you she shampooed my hair yet? Well, over and over and over again. Now tell me something, is it just me—I really like being shampooed without listening to the stylists talk to one another at the shampoo bowls. In my opinion, silence is golden at this particular time because there are clients who really just look forward to the shampoo only because it's relaxing and it can feel like a massage even if you are not giving one. I was unable to take that short trip in my mind, so I listened to what happened yesterday in another stylist's home even if I did not want to listen. It really would have been nice to visit Italy for a minute and enjoy a nice glass of wine in my mind while listening to the pianist play a soothing melody of any great song and let tranquility take its place. Not today!

After returning to my chair after the loong shampoo I was asked how I wanted my hair styled. One thing that attracted me to her, and you already know where I'm going with this, was that she specialized in healthy hair. If I cannot remember anything else a stylist tells me, this is one line that I can remember, because it is important. She actually did a good job on my hair and I left out swinging my hair! It had so much body. I love wearing my hair down and when it's down it should be movable, even when you turn your head. Now you know your hair looks good when you go to work the next day and everyone makes a comment on how beautiful it looks. So here I go again with my famous statement: I found my stylist. WRONG!

Next visit, day before my birthday celebration! I've heard the old saying, "You are over the hill" when you reach a certain age, but believe me, I'm standing on top in full force, so don't even start with the age.

Here's my story: Before going, I picked up my sister at the airport. She flew in for the birthday celebration and decided she wanted to go along with me and possibly get her hair done as well, so I called while on the way and my stylist recommended another stylist in the shop since she was booked, which is definitely understandable.

We got there and waited for at least 30 minutes and finally she called me back, but she had another stylist wash my hair so she could continue to work on another client. I went to the shampoo bowl and she started…

You know what, everyone? My head is starting to tingle just thinking about writing about how she tortured my scalp with her fingernails! She scratchpooed my hair and scalp. (Yes, that is my new word I'm adding to my dictionary.) I just did not understand this. How could you do someone's head like this! I was ready to get up by the time she started and she knew that right away.

When I got back to my stylist's chair and she started to comb my hair, it was completely tangled! My stylist knew immediately that I was upset. She had a difficult time untangling my hair, and I told her if she couldn't shampoo my hair, no one could. Now I know there are shampooers in some shops who are fine and shampoo very well, but no…not the Nail Drillers, please. My hair hasn't been that tangled since I had an afro! Now if you can tangle straight hair that bad, you are a tough sister.

There is a technique to shampooing hair and if you don't know, you need to ask somebody. Hey, why not me! Shampooing longer hair, you must not have it going in every direction. You can have the hair hanging downward and the movement of your hands going the same way too.

After the untangling and the drying of my hair were completed, she proceeded to flat-iron my hair. To make a long story short, my hair was a disaster! She did not have my hair like it was on my first visit, which was flawless. This time it was less the flaw. I had to work with my hair that night for it to look good the next day for the celebration. I was so disappointed and still today this lady has not called me to check on why I haven't been back. Now you know this really bothers me.

6

Tear-Jerking Cut

WHAT A TITLE, but this next story earned its name.

This patron, Mishal, came to work distraught from her hair being cut drastically. I recall when she left work on Tuesday it was shoulder length. Recently she had a trim and had been growing her hair back. She already had in her mind by July her hair would be long enough for a certain style she wanted to wear with her attire for a special function /family reunion.

Now you know we all look forward to seeing loved ones we haven't seen in years and we want to make sure we are looking good. This is just a natural thing.

Well, she got in the chair and got a relaxer; after the stylist washed her hair and brought her back to the chair, she combed her hair straight down and Mishal could see that her hair had grown even more and was pleased to know that the style she was anticipating would definitely work out. The stylist said she had a few dead ends and she would trim them off, even though Mishal knew it couldn't be too bad since she'd had a good trim seven weeks prior. Well, here we go again.

The patron was turned away from the mirror and the stylist started her trimming. After she finished she turned Mishal to the mirror and her hair had been cut off at least six inches. That's a lot!

Immediately Mishal was upset and her eyes started to tear up. She asked her, "Why did you cut my hair off?" The stylist's reply: "Well, there were several dead ends that needed to be cut." What Mishal did not realize was that the stylist kept going over her trim several times. Why? Now I know you are not asking me this question!

Okay, here goes: She screwed up, point-blank. Sorry, I had to go there again because this is one of the number one stories that deals with cutting/trimming. I empathize with what Mishal has gone through. She went from excitement from her hair growing to dismay real quick. Her hair had been taken away within minutes. Now my eyes are tearing up; okay, I must go on and get myself back together in order to continue with my stories. I have become very sensitive to hair stories of this nature.

If you are a patron and reading this book, listen to me and listen well. When you sit in a stylist's chair let her know immediately, even before she touches your hair, that you do not want your hair cut off, and if it needs to be trimmed, you tell her exactly how many inches. It's your hair and when you have had so many bad experiences with hair being cut instead of trimmed, it is necessary to be adamant about what you want.

7

My Journey Continues (2009)

A LADY I know referred me to a salon in the neighborhood that I actually have visited before but used another stylist who is no longer there. This stylist was highly recommended by the owner. The day of my appointment, I was greeted with a smile by the owner of this beautiful building, which was actually in the process of being remodeled. When I was there a few years ago I thought it was already stunning, but after walking around with the owner, I found that they were making it bigger and better. I thought to myself, this is the type of environment anyone would love to be in.

I forgot to mention that the stylist called me earlier in the day to remind me of my appointment, and that really impressed me, because if a client has forgotten or plans have changed, this is the time to inform the stylist. This lady was raking in points already and I hadn't made it there yet.

She also greeted me with a smile and told me that she did promote healthy hair, and you already know where I'm going next—healthy hair! That's the first step to falling in love with my stylist. She told me what products she used for relaxing and she applied the relaxer perfectly. The shampoo was magnificent! She massaged my scalp and there were no nails digging into my skull. Now that I think about it, when the other person shampooed my hair, it actually felt like her nails pierced my scalp and she touched the actual bone structure of my skull—now that was deep, literally.

The end result from this visit—completely satisfied! My hair was soft and movable while shining like new money.

I'm preparing at this moment to set up another appointment for a wash and set. Now you know the problem I've had was the second visit not comparing to the first. Tune in next week for the results.

Next week arrived and I made my second appointment. Well, guess what, I was satisfied again. This could be contagious, I was hoping. You know, we communicated in regards to my last appointment and I was glad to tell her how many compliments I had on my hair at my class reunion. She was so happy to hear that. She even told me that she had a new technique she wanted to try on my hair that she had just learned at a hair show that had workshops. I was so happy to hear that she wanted to stay on top of all new products and styles by attending hair functions while also participating.

Since she already knew that I prefer wearing my hair down, it was the perfect style for me and the technique that was used to insure that my hair would flow did exactly what she said it would do.

Hey, I'm here at work now, turning my head from left to right just to feel the movement, and for a minute I thought my hair wrapped around my face twice because it was flowing just that good. Okay, let me stop, I'm getting a little carried away and a cramp in my neck.

You know, as a satisfied customer, I can't help but tip and give praises. Looks like I may have a keeper, and we will know before I end this book.

8

The Magnificent Stylist

AS YOU ALREADY know I had the opportunity to visit my hometown recently and was able to spend some time with my sister in-law Cynlia. We sat down to chat and she told me about one of the most highly rated stylist I have ever heard of yet. "She is magnificent!" Cynlia said with a big smile on her face. This is how she operates:

- Chair is guaranteed to be waiting for you upon arrival.
- No one can talk with her when she has a client.
- Communicates on how hair is progressing.
- Never cuts your hair unless requested.
- Promotes healthy hair.
- Has certain product you can purchase that are used on hair.
- Products are applied correctly.
- After shampoo, massage is given, and not a quick one.
- She gives "Customer Appreciation" coupons to patrons toward percentage off hair appointments annually.
- Does not overbook. Clients are spread out.
- Advance notice given upon taking vacation.

There were so many good things about this person and no negatives, which rated her as a class act. On my next visit to the Rock, I needed to at least peek in and get a glimpse of her and how she operated, and I was guessing, if I needed to actually speak with her, an appointment would have to be made. No problem with me on that. I could respect a person like this.

Are there any more? Sure, but it definitely takes time to venture out and find them. I have to use the word venture because that's what it feels like when you are out searching constantly. You never know what you're going to get. Remember Forrest Gump and the phrase "Life is like a box of chocolates"? Well, whenever I get an assortment of chocolates, I end up throwing most of them away, and finding a hair stylist should not be that way.

9

My Journey Continues

WELL, MY KEEPER could not be kept any longer, or I might just keep her on standby, just in case. I know you are waiting to find out what happened. Now this may be minor to you, but I cannot take a lot of talking to other people across the room; it's annoying and takes away my time. With all the distractions, my hair was nothing like it should have been from previous visits and I haven't returned. Her attention to others resulted in another unsatisfied client.

I have actually come to the conclusion regarding several stylists that when it comes to chemical services, mostly relaxers, we want to rush through it without applying it correctly. I came across another stylist again who I thought was applying base, and all the time it was a relaxer. This last stylist I saw actually parted my hair and placed the relaxer on my scalp as if she were oiling my scalp. She also applied more on my already relaxed hair, which can cause breakage and over processing, actually making hair weak and with no elasticity. So, since I only have one head of hair, I have stopped my visits indefinitely. The journey has ended for now. Isn't this sad?

I know you are thinking, how could I go so long from chair to chair? Well, I really like to be pampered, and I want someone to assist in taking care of my hair. I've reached a certain age, and I deserve a break. Can anyone out there take on the challenge and the same for others who are in my situation? I know you are out there but I can't find you, so will you come and reach out to us?

I was really hoping I wouldn't get to the plea part, but when a woman is fed up in more ways than one, it's a challenge bringing her back.

There were several things I liked about the last stylist, who I visited at least three times. The chair was always waiting upon my arrival, she was pleasant and didn't talk much so that I could experience my special time, and I was in and out without being there half the day. She could trim/cut hair perfectly, but the relaxing technique was the big part that bothered me as I mentioned earlier. Do some stylists need to be retrained on applying relaxers? Relaxers and perms are chemical processes and should be taken seriously.

Now how would it sound if I told her, "When you apply the relaxer, can you focus on the new growth only?" Some stylists do not want you telling them how to do their work, but some need to be told. Maybe I need to go back to cosmetology school and see if the procedure for applying relaxer has changed, just in case I'm wrong, but I don't think so! I just can't give in to that.

When over processing takes place, the hair starts breaking and shedding, and this is exactly what happened to me. Even without over processing, chemicals are harsh on the hair, period, so let's not add to it. From this point on, I'm taking care of my own hair, but first, treatment must take place to get my hair healthy again.

I recently spoke with my sister who resides in Arkansas, and she stated that she has made up her mind to come and have me do her hair. This means she is flying from another state just to have her hair relaxed and cut correctly. She has experienced over processing as well. She was also a hair stylist at one time, so she has experienced the same problems I have. This is so sad. What is going on out there? Have we decided to make up our own techniques, which, may I add, are not working? I have finally figured out why the wig and weave business is booming. We have unhealthy, damaged, or no hair at all. This is upsetting.

10

Weaves

WEAVES HAVE COME to the rescue for a lot of us. Don't get me wrong, there is nothing like a good weave, but a bad one can be a disaster. I'm sure clients come in with hair that they have purchased themselves and that could be exactly the right color and texture. Well, what about the ones who don't? Do you go ahead and add it on without being honest? You know I have my suggestion, which is to be up front and honest, because if you inform her that it will not complement her natural hair and she still wants it, then you know you have done your job.

Now, if she says, "Well, what do you suggest?" and you give her the feedback she needs to hear, she may well exchange it or have you purchase it for her. Another thing, you may want to ask clients who do bring hair in if it's feasible for them to come early or the day before to make sure the hair will work for them. This will eliminate having to delay or reschedule if it doesn't. Just my personal suggestion of course, which I think is a good one.

Always keep in mind that every client's hair that you do is representative of you. When she leaves your chair and walks out the door, she is actually advertising your work. Now what results do you get from good advertisement? Yes, you know where I'm going. More clients! Of course if you have enough clients, you may be able to recommend another stylist who does a great job just like you. Hey! Pass the blessings around if you can; they will come right back to you.

11

Natural Hair

AFRICAN AMERICANS WEARING their natural hair have come back in full force. If you haven't noticed already, we are seeing more people wearing their natural hair, which is beautiful! Whether afro, pressed, braided, etc., it has returned. So, stylist, how are we handling our clients who wear their natural hair? They shouldn't be handled any different from others of course.

One concern brought to my attention is the pricing; for example, pressing. How do we determine it—by the length, thickness, etc.? This is something you should consider closely. I know pressing can be time-consuming depending on the length, or curls may need to be added afterward. Just make sure you have a price list visibly posted and be consistent with the price as well. This is true for all hair services. Don't charge one amount and another on the next visit for the same service. I'm just telling you what I'm hearing from others. If you do plan a future price hike, please give patrons plenty of notice.

12

Time Management

STYLISTS, THIS IS a subject that has been mentioned to me by several people I have visited with, and it concerns time. Unless you have a full-service salon that includes manicures/pedicures, waxing, massages, etc., no one should spend over three hours at the salon if they are only there for one service. Please, please, manage your time when scheduling. Who wants to stay in a salon all day?

An owner of a shop approached me who was informed that I had been having problems with finding a stylist and all the issues I was having. She was also aware that I was in the process of writing about my experiences, so she asked that I come and speak with her stylists at her establishment. Apparently she was aware of the problems in her own salon and spa and felt that this would give the newcomers some advice on how to keep a client forever. Well, I think I'm the perfect person for the job, even though I have never done public speaking, but you know what? It's needed. So I am thinking about accepting the invitation.

For the stylist who does a great job and is able to keep clients forever, you need a standing ovation each time a client leaves your chair, that's how much you are appreciated and needed. I'm sorry but I'm very serious about this and it's no laughing matter when your hair has been mistreated. So keep doing what you're doing and pass it along any chance you get.

I could go on and on with stories nonstop, but most of them will be the same stories over and over again that I have heard from patrons, and that is because the issues are consistent.

The following list will assist those who continue to lose clients and really are not sure why. Hopefully this will at least make you think about what we are experiencing as patrons and how much we would love to give our business to you if more caring is shown and procedures are followed when any chemicals are involved, etc.

This list will also put you on your way to building a strong clientele that will be with you forever and will guarantee you a great future in this business. After all, the hair business will never go away.

If you are not even close to following any items on this list, believe me, you will lose clients forever.

13

How to Keep a Client Forever

- Respect clients
- Show professionalism at all times
- Show concern if a client is unhappy about their hair and correct the problem
- Give suggestions on maintaining healthy hair at home
- Communicate to avoid mistakes
- Don't overbook — have the chair waiting
- Apply all chemicals correctly
- Do not over process
- Do not cut hair unless told it's okay — discuss length to cut first!
- Know the difference between a trim versus a cut
- Do not use fingernails when shampooing
- Avoid excessive talking with others
- Focus on the client who's in the chair at all times
- Make follow-up/courtesy calls on new clients
- Know your clients' birthdays
- Give senior citizens a discount

- Conduct a drawing for a free wash and set occasionally
- Have a yearly appreciation party
- Stay updated on new products and styles
- Promote healthy hair at all times

14

How to Lose a Client Forever

- Give poor customer service
- Be poor at communicating / listening
- Show no concern about client hair
- Pay no attention to a dissatisfied client
- Overbook
- Always be late/never on time
- Overprice
- Have a loud tone of voice
- Leave client under dryer for a extended amount of time to do others
- Use profanity
- Over process with any chemicals
- Apply chemicals incorrectly
- Hide a haircut gone wrong
- Do not correct a problem
- Don't do what's best for the client, only for you
- Don't make follow-up calls when new client doesn't return

About the Author

HAZEL L. BOGARD is the mother of three sons. She is the seventh child. Born and raised in Little Rock, Arkansas, she has spent most of her life residing in Dallas, Texas.

She has held a management position for a major commercial real estate company for several years in a customer service environment. Hazel has always been attentive to customer service anywhere she goes. After previously being in the cosmetology field for several years, she felt the need to share her personal experiences regarding customer service and her determination of what good customer service is.

Hazel enjoys writing, music, skating, exercising, dancing, cooking, reading, decorating, traveling, entertaining, and mostly just being herself and enjoying life.